WHO'S
WITH
ME?

WHO'S WITH ME?

The Bible Meets Life-31 days of Practical Christianity

TOBILOBA AJAYI

TATE PUBLISHING
AND ENTERPRISES, LLC

Published by Tate Publishing & Enterprises, LLC
127 E. Trade Center Terrace | Mustang, Oklahoma 73064 USA
1.888.361.9473 | www.tatepublishing.com

Tate Publishing is committed to excellence in the publishing industry. The company reflects the philosophy established by the founders, based on Psalm 68:11,
"The Lord gave the word and great was the company of those who published it."

Book design copyright © 2015 by Tate Publishing, LLC. All rights reserved.
Cover design by Jim Villaflores
Interior design by Mary Jean Archival

Published in the United States of America

ISBN: 978-1-63418-386-4
1. Religion / Biblical Commentary / General
2. Self-Help / Motivational & Inspirational
15.04.08

For Jesus Christ,
the lover of my soul and the giver of the words;
this book is all yours,
I am only a scribe, the highest honour I can ever receive.

Acknowledgments

Thanks to all God's fellow workers who worked, cried, and cheered with me as I learned and scribed the lessons in this book.

Michael Obadan, you prodded and didn't stop till I wrote. Thank you for the deep questions and late-night conversations. You rock.

Sarah Ferron, you asked for a second book and you listened to me whine through the process. I love you.

Adenike Adediran, words are not enough; the world needs more friends like you.

Tolu tope Dada, you taught me about the power of a seed. Here's the harvest of the seed you sowed.

Wale and Sade Irelewuyi, I'm still writing because you thought it was not a crazy idea. Thank you.

Babes Redefined, my Facebook family who kept me writing because they kept reading; I'm hooked.

Yemi and Yvonne Awosanya, "write it down," you said, and I'm still writing. You both rock! Thank you for being so supportive.

'Jide Balogun, brother, friend, mischief partner, and naughty student, you find time out of no time to be there. Thank you.

Oluwamitomisin Somorin, two sentences of timely wisdom and I'm good for weeks. Thank you.

Mr. Bunmi Ajayi, new daddies better come for lessons. I'm blessed to be your daughter. Thank you for sticking with my crazy ideas and supporting them.

RCCG Fountain of Life, thank you for helping me grow by asking the real questions and letting me be me!

RCCG TSP, thank you for challenging me with the never-ending controversies and questions.

Kunle and Kofo Adetola, thank you for being real, being open, and teaching by example. I'll be back for more.

Pastor and Mrs. Momoh, you encouraged this gift every step of the way, and you don't let me give up. I'm grateful.

To all my siblings, thank you for allowing me to stress you with everything from book deliveries to extra luggage stress and costs. I'm blessed beyond measure with you all.

To my nieces and nephews, thank you for those humbling conversations that get me thinking. God does indeed use the foolish things of this world to confound the wise.

The Tate Publishing family, you suggested a blog after my first book, and it has morphed into my second. Thank you for all the support you've given me as a "green" writer. God couldn't have sent me better publishers.

And to you my readers, thank you for taking the time to read this book. Be blessed as you read.

Contents

Introduction

The book you're about to read started as blog posts that I started after a lot of prodding by my publishers and friends while my first book was in publication.

You are about to read a part of what God did when I turned the plan and desire to blog over to Him. He's taught me things and gave me the ability to scribe things that have changed my life as I learned these lessons.

The book is laid out in a devotional format for thirty-one days so that it is easy to read and you can have something to digest for the day.

Some of these things will be as difficult to read and do for you as they were difficult for me to do and write, but I can say with all certainty that what you are about to read has the capacity to change your life completely.

There are a lot of personal-life anecdotes spread throughout the book that I hope you can relate to.

As you read, may your hearts be led to seek the savior, Jesus Christ.

Enjoy!

DAY 1

The Most Misunderstood Love Story

I don't know about you, but I love 'love stories.' I must have read hundreds of Mills & Boon titles by the time I left secondary school.

Any witnesses in the house?

When I gave my life to Christ, that love did not change, so I became a sucker for love stories with Christian themes; the authors could not turn them out fast enough because I have a voracious reading appetite for the popular authors of the genre.

By the way, I have a thing for love notes and love letters too. I'm sure if I search my room well enough, I'll still find some as old as fifteen years ago. (Stop looking at me funny. I know some of you still have them too.)

Why do we like love stories and keep love notes? We reread them over and over, and we can almost quote some of them verbatim with sheepish smiles on our faces.

Why am I going on and on about this? Well I want to tell my own very brief version of a popular love story, and so I'm setting the scene.

Here it goes:

There was once a woman who committed murder. According to the law, she was to be killed. Her execution date was set, and she was cooling her heels in prison awaiting the day.

On the day of her execution, the door to her cell opened, and she was told she's free to go. When she asked why, she was told another person had chosen to die in her place, fulfilling the requirement of the law.

"Who is this person, and what does He want in return or hope to gain from taking my punishment?" she asked.

"I don't know who he is," the jailer answered. "He only asks that I give you this book."

She took the book from the jailer and opened it.

The first page read, "I love you so much. I couldn't let you die. You don't know me yet. That's why I sent you this book. It contains all you need to know about me and more. I hope that in time, you will come to love me back."

It was unsigned.

The end.

What do you think the woman did with the book?

More importantly, what would you do with it if you were that woman?

The characters in the story represent you and I. The woman represents you and I. We've committed sins for which death is the only punishment.

Jesus is the person who took your place so you wouldn't die because He loves you too much. Your Bible is the book, His love letter to you. Only when you study it can you begin to know and understand His heart and His motives.

Read with me: "For God so loved the world that He gave His only Son that whoever believes in Him will not die, but have eternal life" (John 3:16).

It is only when you understand the love story that you can begin to reciprocate the love.

Are you reading your love notes? Are you reading His love story?

Do you understand it?

Are you reciprocating the love?

I need to go back to my love story.

I need to go back to my Bible.

Who's with me?

—Tobiloba

DAY 2

Which Truth?

I was in a Bible study teachers' meeting, and for the first time, I connected two scriptures I have always known in a completely new way.

I'm sure you, Bible scholars, already know this, but pardon my "learner's spirit." I just caught the revelation.

The first scripture reads, "And you shall know the truth and the truth shall set you free" (John 8:32).

I've known this scripture for a while, and I've always asked, "Which truth?" The answer I've always been given is "The Bible, of course."

And the answer was right. But as I continued to grow in my walk with God and in communion with other believers and as I started to hear different interpretations of Scripture, I have to admit I *almost* started to feel like I could not trust the Bible as the source of truth any more.

And then God addressed that issue completely by opening my eyes to the truth in yet another very common scripture. It reads, "I am the way, the truth, and the life. No one comes to the Father except through me" (John 14:6). It suddenly hit me. I need to know the truth. Jesus is the truth. I need no other standard. He is the truth I need. If I truly know Jesus, then I will be set free from the bondage of various doctrines making rounds today. I will not get sidetracked or confused by anyone.

The truth I need is the truth according to Jesus.

The only way to know this truth is to know Jesus himself.

I need to get to know more of Jesus.

Who is with me?

—Tobiloba

DAY 3

Are You Being Pruned?

I was in church and the speaker made reference to a very common scripture that has not let me rest since then. It reads,

> *And He cleanses and repeatedly prunes every branch that continues to bear fruit, to make it bear more and richer and more excellent fruit.*
>
> *You are cleansed and pruned already, because of the word which I have given you [the teachings I have discussed with you].*
>
> *John 15:2–3 (*AMP*)*

I just could not get over the fact that if we are bearing fruit as Christians, they we would have to go through the rigours of dropping the things that are unnecessary and undesirable. That's what pruning is.

Pruning is not interesting. It is painful hard work.

The funny part of it is that pruning is not a onetime thing. It is a continuous process.

If pruning stops, fruit-bearing stops, and the tree eventually dies.

Our pruning instrument is the Word of God (John 15:3).

Therefore every time I study the Word, it should have a pruning effect on me. I should, as a result of reading the Word, drop things that are undesirable in my life from time to time.

If the Word is not having this effect, I'm not being pruned, and my fruit-bearing will be limited.

If this continues, my fruit-bearing will eventually stop, thereby making me a dead tree.

The above applies to you too.

The Word has to have visible effect in my life.

The Word has to prune me.

Who's with me?

—Tobiloba

DAY 4

God Is Your Source

Somehow, I have always worked in jobs that have a pay package that could not pay my bills.

And these jobs were God-given jobs.

For a while on my first job, I wanted to change jobs so badly, especially those days I caught up with a few of my classmates, and I heard the figures they were earning. I was green with envy. They had glamorous lives, went to all the happening places, could afford so many things…I wanted to be "successful" like them.

I begged, cajoled, negotiated—the whole nine yards. God was not going to budge. I was not going to get another job.

At least not from Him.

For a very long time, I could not reconcile the God that I knew who wants me to prosper (3 John 2); with the God who was making me stay in a job that could not even pay my bills not to talk of any extras. I was in this quiet state of discontent until I heard my dad use these words in a prayer session:

"And you shall remember the LORD your God, for *it is* He who gives you power to get wealth" (Deut 8:18, NKJV).

I spent all day thinking about that scripture, and then sometime after that, I heard something that I have never forgotten:

God is your source and He determines your resources. And then it hit me.

Your employers don't. Your profit margin doesn't. Your parents don't. God does.

It does not matter how much you earn or don't earn. God determines your resources because He is your source.

As I nodded in enlightenment, it was almost as if God was saying, "Now you get it."

God provides for what He ordains. Relax. If you're in His will, you'll never be without help.

Ask me. I went four months without pay in God's will, and I did not run into debt. That could only have been God.

Am I advocating staying in jobs that don't pay well when you can get a better one? No chance! Even the Bible says, "Money is a defence" (Eccl 7:12).

I'm just saying, stay in God's will. His provision will meet you there.

By the way, I learned what it truly meant to be successful by the time God was done with that phase.

So if doing what God wants you to do and resources are looking tight, remember, God is your source, and He determines your resources.

Nothing or no one else has that privilege.

Who's with me?

—Tobiloba

DAY 5

God's Got Your Back

In recent times, I looked at my account balance and thought about all the upcoming expenses, and I was worried—so worried it was all I could think about. I thought about it till I was almost depressed. (I'm sure some of you can relate) and then the Holy Spirit said to me,

"Hebrews 13:5."

I flipped my Bible over to the scripture wondering if my mind was playing tricks on me. This is what I found:

> *Keep your lives free from the love of money and be content with what you have, because God has said,*
>   *"Never will I leave you; never will I forsake you."*[1]

I thought, *But it's not like I love money like that. At least God wants me to prosper.* And then it hit me:

The point where I began to worry about money, I contravened a direct command of God not to worry (Philippians 4:6). Money had become more important to me than obeying God.

The minute I start to contemplate working when I should be in God's presence,

The minute I start to contemplate scrimping on my tithes and offering,

I started loving money instead of loving God.

How? You may ask. You see, what you love, you think about. What you love, you pursue. What you love, you sacrifice for. The absence of what you love depresses you.

That last one hit home for me. Lack of money was depressing me. I was becoming in love with money.

The antidote is clear: contentment! To borrow from Joyce Meyer, "Enjoy where you are on the way to where you are going."

Why? God's got my back, and He does not plan to leave me without help. He'll do the same or you.

We just need to trust Him.

The mirror of the Word has just exposed another area where I need help.

I need to learn true contentment.

Lord, teach me contentment in Jesus's name.

Amen!

Who's with me?

—Tobiloba

DAY 6

Trust His Timing, Trust His Vision

I went through a phase recently that has me questioning God. I find myself asking, "What are you doing?"

You see, I see so many things that I perceive as unjust and unfair, and the inequality in life just rubs me off the wrong way. Then to further solidify the need for this post, someone essentially asked the same question in one of the Christian groups that I belong to. In the Holy Spirit's quiet way, this was what He reminded me: "For everything there is a season, a time for every activity under heaven" (Ecclesiastes 3:1).

God is a time-conscious God. He created and controls time. The story of creation clearly illustrates that. Everything was created on a separate day including a day set out to rest.

When we as humans work with time, we do it based on our limited knowledge and insight, but when God works with time, he does it based on His limitless knowledge, hindsight, and foresight.

This obviously translates to differences in the perception of the things that are happening around us.

Think about it. If you had a ten-month-old baby wanting to play with a knife, would you allow it?

Almost all of us would not because we love the child and know that a knife would be harmful. Even if the child started to cry and bang his head against a wall, you would not change your mind. Why?

Your sight is better than the child's own. You can foresee consequences he can't even comprehend.

When it seems like God is not being fair, think about Him the same way. He is a loving parent who sees more than we can ever even imagine. He sees the end of a thing before it even begins, and He wants the best for you and for me.

As a result, He's going to have to say no to some of my requests.

He's going to have to make me wait for some things even if I think I'm ready for them.

He's going to have to allow me go through some painful experiences.

He's going to have to define justice differently than I would sometimes.

Most of us have since realised that all those things we classified as "wicked" when we were growing up was actually training by our parents to equip us for the future.

The time is coming when we will look at the things that seem unfair now, and thank God for them.

But while we still don't get it, what do we do?

We trust his timing and trust His vision.

He has perfect timing and perfect vision.

Who's with me?

—Tobiloba

Don't Just Confess, Repent

There are certain sins in my life that I find myself confessing every day. These things are just daily struggles.

If you don't have anything like that in your life, I thank God for you (I want to be like you when I grow up).

But if you're like me and there's something that you find yourself confessing every time you pray, read on.

I was just going about my day when the following words started to haunt me:

"Repent, for the kingdom of God is at hand" (Mathew 3:2).

I am saved, sanctified, and sealed, so I knew the message was beyond giving my life to Christ. As I began to ponder and ask God what He meant, this is what I've learned:

The reason I'm confessing a particular issue all the time is that I am not repenting of the issues I am confessing. My confessions are sincere, but I am not repenting.

What does it mean to repent? The Amplified Bible puts it this way: "*Repent (think differently; change your mind, regretting your sins and changing your conduct),* for the kingdom of heaven is at hand."

Therefore, with repentance, it's not just enough to be say, "I'm sorry for my sin; my conduct has to change. For my conduct to change, the way I think about my sin must change. I need to see sin the way God sees it."

If all I'm doing is confessing and not repenting, my salvation is on shaky ground.

Repentance takes work. I have to consciously choose to change my thoughts and subsequently my actions in the areas I'm constantly confessing.

I need to stop giving excuses.

The mirror of the word has just exposed another blemish.

God! Help your daughter!

Who's with me?

—Tobiloba

DAY 8

Confess Your Sins...to One Another

I was in a prayer service one day, and the prayer leader was urging us all to pray. While doing this, he said, quoting from the Bible, "The effectual fervent prayer of a righteous man availeth much" Pray, my brethren, pray.

While the voices in the auditorium increased in volume, my mind was stuck on the Bible quotation above. I got home and I looked it up. Maybe I shouldn't have because since that day, I have not gotten over what I discovered.

You see, I discovered that like it's commonly done, only one-half of that scripture was emphasised, and this was the part usually used in prayer sessions. We tend to ignore the first part of the verse, which reads,

"Confess your sins to one another and pray for one another that you may be healed."

I have to admit, we are good at the "praying for one another" bit, but we tend to selectively forget to "confess our sins to one another."

I notice it does not say to confess only to a priest or a pastor or an elder. It says, "each other," meaning your fellow brother or sister in the Lord.

Unfortunately that scripture puts everything together in one equation. *Confession of sins to other believers + prayer by same believers = healing*

How sweet would it be if believers would all obey this instruction?

When someone admits an area of sin in their lives to you, it's not time to judge them; it's time to obey the scripture and pray for them.

But how many of us, I included, would not judge them first?

I'm wondering aloud how many healings we've delayed or are still delaying because we are practicing selective obedience.

Hmm, this is serious! God, I need your help.

Lord, your church needs help! Help us to obey you completely in this area, even if it means starting with our small core groups and not just assume it's impossible. Amen!

—Tobiloba

DAY 9

Love, Not Fear

It's a very common occurrence to hear a single Christian girl say about her dream man: "He must fear God."

I subscribed to that line of thought until a scripture I thought I understood struck me in a new light. Here it is:

> We know how much God loves us, and we have put our trust in his love.
>
> God is love, and all who live in love live in God, and God lives in them. And as we live in God, our love grows more perfect. So we will not be afraid on the Day of Judgment, but we can face him with confidence because we live like Jesus here in this world.
>
> Such love has no fear, because perfect love expels all fear. If we are afraid, it is for fear of punishment, and this shows that we have not fully experienced his perfect love.[1]

I've found myself pondering this scripture, and the more I ponder, the more amazed I get.

The one thing that God values above all things is love because that's who He is. Love is not what God does. It is who He is.

As a result, that's how God wants us to live. He wants us to live in love, not in fear. Everything we do for God should be motivated out of our love for Him and not our fear of Him.

Fear and love cannot coexist. If you're operating in fear, you cannot be operating in love. If you're truly operating in love, fear should be out of the window.

Loving God is the access to heaven because it automatically means that we would have lived just like Jesus.

No wonder Jesus constantly admonished His disciples to love Him.

Love will lead to willful obedience while fear leads to compelled obedience.

Which one do you think God's looking for?

Think about it. When you truly love someone, your sacrifices for them are joyful and spontaneous, and you go out of your way to make them smile (to name a few of the things we do for love). Serving them is a joy not a duty. Doing anything out of fear has the exact opposite effect.

God wants your love and not your fear.

If you truly love God, you would not need to fear him.

My love for God needs to deepen!

Who's with me!

—Tobiloba

DAY 10

Is Love Enough?

I don't know about you, but over the years, I've heard the phrase "Love is not enough to keep a marriage"—even from pastors, and I'd honestly come to believe it.

Until one night.

I was in one of my very argumentative moods with the Holy Spirit, and we were talking relationships and marriage—again, and in supporting one of my arguments, I said, "But, God, love is not enough to keep a marriage."

And then as usual, God stopped me cold in my tracks with His response: "You mean, I'm not enough to keep a marriage?"

I stopped cold. Then the Holy Spirit went on and reminded me of a scripture I've known since I was a child:

Read with me: "The person who refuses to love does not know the first thing about God because God is love" (1 John 4:8, MSG).

Of course the punch line was "God is love."

The lesson continued: If you say love is not enough to keep a marriage, then you are saying I'm not enough to keep a marriage.

All the connotations of love are found in me. Romantic, familial and even friendships. You need all the permutations of love to keep a marriage; therefore, I'm the one you need.

One permutation of love, romantic love for instance, will not keep a marriage, but the God kind of love will. (All permutations) End of lesson.

Question (God): Is love enough to keep a marriage?

Answer (me mumbling, after eating humble pie): Yes.

The God kind of love is all I need to make a marriage work because that kind of love is God Himself!

I need to renew my mind and cultivate the God kind of love!

Who's with me?

—Tobiloba

DAY 11

Is Divorce Really the Answer?

"I cannot believe you cheated on me! With someone I know too. That's it. We're done! I'm getting a divorce. I cannot stand the sight of your cheating face around me anymore," he/she says, storming out of the room.

A few minutes later, he/she is narrating the story in fury to a friend who says, "You can't get divorced, remember? You're a Christian."

"Well, the Bible does say I can divorce an unfaithful husband/wife, and it will not be a sin,[2] so I'm taking that option. It's better than living with someone who cheated on me."

But is divorce really the answer for unfaithfulness in Christian marriages? The Bible tells us that the relationship between a man and his wife is likened to the relationship between Christ and the Church.[3]

We are the church of Christ—his bride. If Christ took the option of divorce every single time that we were unfaithful to Him, would any of us be able to stand? Check your life! In the last twenty-four hours, if you're like me, I'm sure you can find more than one instance of unfaithfulness to Christ to point to. But does Christ turn his back (divorce) on me every time I commit an indiscretion and break His heart, disrespect His body, and scorn His sacrifice?

No! He forgives me and keeps forgiving me every time I acknowledge my sin and go to Him for help. What's more? He helps me to truly repent of my sin by covering my sin with His grace.

Could we take a cue from Christ and bring an extension of the forgiveness and grace we have received from Christ into our marriages even in the face of infidelity?

Is divorce really the answer?

I don't think so?

Who's with me?

—Tobiloba

DAY 12

No Marriage Is Beyond Saving

The first time I shared yesterday's study on divorce, where I advocated forgiveness even when divorce is an option—a biblical one at that—I got a lot of questions and opinions that sent me to my knees and back to the Word.

I realize that majority of us consciously or unconsciously believe that there are certain lines in marriage that once crossed there's no coming back from. I was told that even Jesus must have recognized that possibility. He allows divorce on the condition of adultery.[1]

I have to say that argument was quite convincing to my human mind. I mean it makes sense. But I have come to realize that a lawful concession does not always mean beneficial agreement.

I know a lot of people will disagree with some or all of the things I'm about to say; that's fine. I'm going to go ahead and obey God anyway. My discoveries of late are below:

Divorce was never part of God's plan when He created marriage. It was a man-made concession because human beings became too hard-hearted and refused to offer forgiveness when they were wronged by their spouses.[2]

When Jesus ratified the concession, He allowed only one ground for divorce, adultery, and then followed it up with a condition that essentially translates to celibacy unless you reconciled to your spouse.[3]

You see the reason for that condition after the ratification continued to baffle me because I felt that God was asking too much. I essentially found myself asking, "If you would allow them to divorce, why would you tell them to stay unmarried unless they reconciled to the spouse you allowed them to divorce in the first place?"

I have now realized that as with everything God does, that condition was put there to help us see that no matter how much we think we know, His plan is ultimately and always better.

Am I saying that spouses do not do unspeakable things to each other in marriage? Of course not. I've heard and seen certain things done to people in the name of marriage (e.g., flagrant adultery, physical abuse, emotional abuse). If I were to judge some of these things by human intellect, crucifixion would be too good a death for some of the perpetrators.

But like I said, God's so much smarter than I am.

TOBILOBA AJAYI

So what should the Christian response be in the cases above and others like them?

These are my practical thoughts after lots of studying and asking.

If you're married to a serial adulterer, please move out of the house before you get a disease. Keep praying for him/her, and if possible, still do other "marital" duties. Prayer not only has the power to completely transform your husband/wife, it ensures that it is impossible for you to hate him/her.

If you're in a physically or an emotionally abusive marriage, get out of there before you get yourself killed. Keep praying for him/her from wherever you are. If he/she is the stalker type, fly under the radar please. Your life is very important.

However, do not stop praying for him/her.

If your marriage was founded on deceit (or they jazzed you like they say where I come from) and the truth comes out, take some time away if you must, but while you are away, pray, pray, and pray! Then you will be able to forgive him/her and continue the marriage.

God created marriages to last, no matter the problems it may encounter on its way.

Marriage God's way takes work. A good marriage is not going to fall out of heaven no matter how "spiritual" you are or how many principles you follow. You are going to have to work at it.

By the way, after I finished this study, I *almost* agree with the disciples.[4]

If you don't have a problem "working out your salvation" (as free as it), why do you think bailing out of your marriage when it has challenges is the only solution?

One last thing to address before I finish, I've heard people advice women especially to stay in a house where they are being abused just so that another woman does not take her place.

I beg you, don't do that! If he marries another woman, is that the end of the story in God's books? I don't think so. I've seen God bring marriages back from worse.

This is the summary of this epistle: no marriage is beyond saving. NO MARRIAGE!

Instead of heading to the courts, why don't we head to the cross?

I'm almost afraid to ask, but

Who's with me?

—Tobiloba

DAY 13

Fruit before Gifts

Have you ever met a Christian—pastor or not—who preaches, teaches, speaks in tongues, works miracles, etc., but has questionable character traits, but you keep getting blown away by the gifts of the Spirit they manifest on a daily basis, especially in these days of church (with emphasis on the gifts of the Holy Spirit)?

If you've not, lucky you. You see, I have. So many times. And I've found myself excusing the questionable behavior in my mind saying, "Who am I to judge a man/woman of God? God decided to use them so they cannot be that bad."

Then recently God started to remind me and show me that in His books, *its fruit before gifts.* It does not matter how many gifts of the Spirit you operate in. If you are not manifesting the fruit of the Spirit, you are on your way to hell.

The Message Bible puts it this way, and I could not have said it better:

> Be wary of false preachers who smile a lot, dripping with practiced sincerity. Chances are they are out to rip you off some way or other. *Don't be impressed with charisma; look for character. Who preachers are is the main thing, not what they say.* A genuine leader will never exploit your emotions or your pocketbook. These diseased trees with their bad apples are going to be chopped down and burned.
>
> Knowing the correct password—saying 'Master, Master,' for instance—isn't going to get you anywhere with me. *What is required is serious obedience—doing what my Father wills.* I can see it now—at the Final Judgment thousands strutting up to me and saying, 'Master, we preached the Message, we bashed the demons, our God-sponsored projects had everyone talking.' And do you know what I am going to say? 'You missed the boat. All you did was use me to make yourselves important. You don't impress me one bit. You're out of here.[1]

What I realised is this when God gives gifts, they are gifts. He does not take them back because we misbehave.[2]

So where does this leave us?

The fact that you are manifesting the gifts does not make you automatically heaven bound. You could be speaking in tongues and on your way to hell.

TOBILOBA AJAYI

By the way, that person I described above could easily be me or you. So while manifesting the gifts, I've learned to focus more on the real deal—the fruit.

Galatians 5:22 gives me a full list. A look at that list reminds me again that I need God.

I am so not there yet.

Lesson learned: The gifts are useless without the fruit. What's the use of the gifts if I use them and end in hell?

Let's focus on the real deal. Cultivate the fruit before the gifts, so help me God. Amen!

Who's with me?

—Tobiloba

DAY 14

The Most Important Fruit

concluded by saying that without the fruit of the Spirit, the gifts did not amount to much.

But my pondering did not stop there. I had a very interesting conversation with a friend about the importance of the fruit and how it was so not easy to live up to the Galatians 5:22 lists.

As the conversation progressed, we discovered certain things (iron sharpening iron) that I just have to share. It's a pretty amazing discovery. I promise. Here it goes:

In every translation of the Bible, Galatians 5:22 always talks about the "fruit" of the Spirit in singular form and then goes on to list nine things (go on and check if you need confirmation). That fact always kind of stumped me, but I agreed with the majority of Christians that this was deliberate because God wanted to let us know that we could not manifest one fruit of the spirit and leave out the other; it is all or nothing.

I have come to discover in recent times that all that we need as Christians is a single fruit of the Spirit. Once we can manifest that single fruit, the rest would be covered. Therefore the use of the singular form 'fruit' is apt.

Before I get accusations of blasphemy, hear me out.

The single fruit you need is LOVE. If we can truly love each other, the requirements of the remaining eight fruit would have been satisfied. Don't take my word for it? Read up 1 Corinthians 4:3–7.

Let me shock you some more. This single fruit trumps every single gift. First Corinthians 12–13:3 points that out. And to cap it all, this singular fruit summarizes the entire law in Mathew 22:40.

If I can love God's way, then I'm good to go.

Loving God's way is so not an emotion. It is a God-backed decision.

It makes me just like Jesus.

And my flesh is going to fight it!

I'm going back to the prayer I borrowed from Joyce Meyer a while ago, and I've stopped praying,

"Lord, reduce me to love!"

Who's with me?

—Tobiloba

DAY 15

The Blessing

You are already blessed!

When we hear of someone being blessed, we think of physical possessions and things that can be seen with the physical eye or perceived with the senses.

A careful reading of the first blessing pronounced on man in Scripture in Genesis 1:28 shows that man was not even physically present.

Man was not formed until Genesis 2:7 after the blessing had been pronounced.

The blessing was not physical. It only manifested in the fullness of time when the man was ready to walk in it.

"As a believer, you have every spiritual blessing you need" (Ephesians 1:3).

If they have not physically manifested, it is not because they do not exist. It is because the time is not yet right for you to walk in them.

When you are ready to walk in it, the exact blessing you need will manifest.

You don't need to ask for what you already have.

While you're waiting for the manifestation of the blessing, ask God to form you completely that you will be ready to walk in to the manifestation of the blessing that you require at every point in time.

I need to stop asking for what I already have.

I am already blessed.

Who's with me?

—Tobiloba

DAY 16

Work Your Blessing

Yesterday we established that the blessing is spiritual. As I continued to meditate on the concept of "The Blessing," my mind was directed to yet another popular scripture. The scripture reads: "The blessing of the LORD makes *one* rich, and He adds no sorrow with it." (Proverbs 10:22).

A reading of the above scripture makes it clear that the blessing of God is in no way money or physical possessions. The blessing is the conveyor of the riches, not riches itself. How does that work? You may ask. Don't worry those were the same questions I asked myself.

And this was the response: "Whatever your hands find to do, do it with all your heart" (Eccl 9:10).

The blessing being spiritual rests on your work. The blessing added to your work brings riches—not just riches but the riches that last.

The blessing will make you rich, but you have to work it.

Go to work. Give your blessing something to rest on and multiply.

The blessing is not money but when added to work makes one rich.

Your inherent blessing+ your work= riches.

That's enough motivation to send me to work every day.

I'm working my blessing.

Who is with me?

—Tobiloba

DAY 17

Just Be a Witness

I was wondering what to write about one day, and this part of a very popular scripture dropped into my mind:

"...and you shall be my witnesses, in Judea, in Samaria and to the ends of the earth" (Acts 1:8).

Christ calls us to simply be witnesses, but unfortunately we've turned ourselves into defense attorneys trying to convince a judge or a jury of our peers.

Am I losing you a little with the legal analogies? Bear with me. I'll find you in a second.

You see, in law, a witness has only one job: tell the court what he or she has seen, heard, or experienced. You can only be an effective witness if you have direct information about a case. In most cases, third-party information, things you were told, is regarded in law as inadmissible hearsay.

The case here is Jesus. How much of direct information do you have about Him? Or is all the information you have "inadmissible hearsay"?

It is not the job or business of the witness to make the judge or the jury believe him. All he has to do is state the facts as he knows them. It is the job of the advocate that called the witness to use the witness's statement(s) to convince the court.

As a Christian, your job ends at stating the fact as you know them. It is not your job to convince anyone of the authenticity or otherwise of the facts you've stated.

That's the job of the Holy Spirit. He's the one that is called "the Advocate."

I've erroneously spent too much time trying to be both witness and advocate.

That's why evangelism has been so hard.

That's why I keep feeling like I'm failing.

I need to stick to my job description.

I need to just be a witness.

Who's with me?

—Tobiloba

DAY 18

Amplify Christ

I have heard it being said in a church workers meeting that the church today is in a sense "recycling" members.

This basically connotes that unbelievers are not joining the fold in the numbers that they should. The current believers are just moving from congregation to congregation.

Then the question of what to do was thrown to the whole house. More evangelism was suggested, radical approaches put forward.

Then recently, I found myself pondering on that discussion, and the Holy Spirit dropped a verse of Scripture in my spirit. It reads, "And I, if and when I am lifted up from the earth [on the cross], will draw and attract all men [Gentiles as well as Jews] to Myself" (John 12:32, AMP).

It is not our job as believers to convert or convince anyone. It is the Holy Spirit's job.

We however have to ensure that our message when we "witness" or "evangelize" is the right message. The right message is a message that has Christ not just as the central theme but as the entire subject matter.

Are you preaching Christ or preaching denominational doctrine and dogma?

Any message that does not preach Christ and Christ only cannot be used by the Holy Spirit to convict or convert anyone.

I dare say that this is the reason our evangelism tactics and crusades and all our programmes toward soul-winning are bearing little to no fruit.

It is only when Christ is lifted up that He can draw men to Himself.

Are we lifting up Christ or our congregations or general overseers?

We need to amplify Christ and nothing else. When we do this, He'll do the rest.

I'm amplifying Christ and Christ only.

Who's with me?

—Tobiloba

Put Grace to Work

It has become a common phenomenon to hear Christians say correctly, "I am under the dispensation of grace," and use that as license to get away with anything. The most deceptive line I've heard and used is "I'm not Jesus, so I *cannot* be perfect."

I was preparing to teach a lesson and I discovered contrary to popular belief that grace does not reduce our responsibility for right living; it increases it.

Before you crucify me, follow me to Matthew 5.[1] Jesus the giver of grace himself tells us that under grace,

1. calling someone a fool could lead you to hell;
2. refusing to pursue peace means unacceptable offerings;
3. lust is equal adultery;
4. swearing oaths are forbidden;

5. remarriage after divorce is adultery;
6. you have to love your enemy;
7. expunge revenge from your dictionary; and
8. perfection is the goal.

This is an impossible list you may say. I know…I used to think like that too until I was reminded this:

Everything that goes into a life of pleasing God has been miraculously given to us by getting to know, personally and intimately, the One who invited us to God—the best invitation we ever received![2]

When Jesus came and died, He not only gave me access to salvation. He also gave me access to His perfection and the ability to live it out.

I can be perfect!

You can be perfect.

I just need to put the grace that Jesus gives me to work by cultivating an intimate personal knowledge of God.

Grace raises the standard, but it also increases the capacity.

I need to put the grace of God in my life to work and stop being lazy.

I need to be able to say like Paul, "I'm not going to let God's grace go to waste."[3]

Who's with me?

—Tobiloba

DAY 20

Allow Peace

I have always had an issue with worry. I used to make a joke that if they handed out degrees based on a person's ability to worry, I would be on my way to getting a PhD by now if I didn't have one.

Don't get me wrong. I know and I've taught that worry is a sin (Philippians 4:6). When God told us not to worry, He was not joking. He meant it. Every time I consciously or unconsciously flout that instruction, I commit a sin.

I keep confessing and asking for forgiveness for this particular issue, but I never fully repented from it. This was one of the issues I alluded to previously.

I was not repenting because I didn't know how to do it. Trust me, I really wanted to repent, but I did not know how to *not* worry. I know prayer works, but some worry sessions were still seeping through the prayer cracks. Why?

Can anyone relate? If you can, keep reading.

Here's what I found recently.

Peace is the antithesis of worry. I cannot worry and have peace. Fortunately when Christ died, He gave me His peace—perfect peace (John 14:27).

Then why was I not walking in the peace that became mine the day Jesus became my Lord and Saviour?

This is what I found in Colossians 3:15 (AMP): "And let the peace (soul harmony which comes) from Christ rule (act as umpire continually) in your hearts [deciding and settling with finality all questions that arise in your minds]."

To have peace, I had to allow peace. I have to choose to let the peace, which Christ has given me, be the default setting of my emotions, and I should always choose to remain in this default setting.

Peace is already available, but I have to choose it.

Worry is a choice. I can choose to worry or *not* worry.

You can make that choice too.

There are two choices: worry or peace. Each of them is knocking at the door of my mind, and I can only allow one.

I choose to allow peace.

Who's with me?

—Tobiloba

Trials Are Good for You

I've been thinking over a portion of scripture for the past two days now, and I've come to the not-so interesting conclusion that as far as God is concerned: trials are good things.

Before you crucify me, read this with me: "Consider it a sheer gift, friends, when tests and challenges come at you from all sides. You know that under pressure, your faith-life is forced into the open and shows its true colours. So don't try to get out of anything prematurely. Let it do its work so you become mature and well-developed, not deficient in any way" (James 1:2–4, MSG).

Trials are not necessarily darts of the enemy that is trying to kill you. In any case, if you are a believer, nothing will come to you that has not first been through God (Colossians 3:3).

Trials are allowed by God to expose the true nature of your faith to you. God uses trials to show you areas where you need to grow and He uses the trials to mature you.

The same way you would allow your child to go through certain things because they need to learn a lesson from it.

Trials work in us to make us more like Jesus.

Trials have a set time frame to complete its work. Don't try to get out of the oven too early, or you may end up half baked.

The fully baked mature Christian must go through trials and complete the course.

I'm learning lessons and growing through my trials.

Who's with me?

—Tobiloba

DAY 22

Living Sacrifices

I've been pondering on a scripture, and I just realised a funny grammatical fact. It contains an oxymoron (two words with opposite meanings used together). Here it is:

> Therefore, I urge you, brothers and sisters, in view of God's mercy, to offer your bodies as a **living sacrifice**, holy and pleasing to God—this is your true and proper worship.[1]

The term *living sacrifice* is the oxymoron, just in case you're still wondering.

This verse just won't let me rest, so here are my discoveries:

The first word that strikes me is the word *offer*. Other translations of the Bible use the word *present*. It still has the same effect. It denotes a choice on the part of the offeror/presenter to give something.

What are we to give? Our bodies. I've wondered why it's not our spirit that should be the offering, and this is what I've discovered: Our bodies are the physical representation of Christ on earth, and He wants us to give it back to Him.[2]

How are we to give it? As living sacrifices. I called these two words an oxymoron earlier, and I'll explain now. A sacrifice is usually dead. It has no will and cannot decide its fate.

Think about it. If you're offering an animal as a sacrifice, it is killed before it is offered.

Yet God wants us to be sacrifices that are alive, meaning we willingly go to the altar and lay aside our choices, our will, our desires, and our ability to decide our fate.

Ouch! That's going to hurt! Badly! That's why it's called a sacrifice. If you're not hurting, you're not yet sacrificing.

You see, the problem with living sacrifices is that they can crawl off the altar. It takes more than human will to keep them there.

If I'm going to remain on God's alter as a living sacrifice, I need to consciously choose to do so and ask God to help me.

It is when I do this that I have begun to truly and properly worship God

I need to crawl back to the altar. I need to remain a living sacrifice.

Lord Help!

Who's with me?

—Tobiloba

DAY 23

Costly Giving

In the last couple of days, I've been going through what I now think is "growing pains." The area of pain has been in giving.

When you see giving, the first thing that comes to mind is money right? Yeah, I know. Before now, I would have thought so too.

God asked me to do something that every iota of my right thinking mind thought was completely crazy. It did not involve money.

I kept thinking, Lord you're asking way too much of me. This is so unfair. And more importantly Lord, how does this benefit me?

Then God sent me to this scripture: "Give away your life, you'll find life given back...Giving not getting is the way." (Luke 6:37–38, MSG).

And then I realised something big.

Giving away our possessions (things) can be easy. But giving ourselves, that's hard.

Giving yourself will cost you! It will hurt! It will be hard.

Until this wake up call, I gave comfortably—offerings, tithes. I even gave my possessions sometimes. But they were not costing me anymore.

As you grow in God, the things that cost you will change. Hence the things that God will demand of you will also change.

God just woke me up. The God kind of giving will cost me! If it's not costing me, I've been giving on my terms not God's.

How are you giving? On your terms or God's terms?

Is your giving costing you?

We need to be like David who said, "I will not offer to the Lord what costs me nothing" (2 Samuel 24:24, 1 Chronicles 21:24).

Examine your giving to God Is it costing you something?

Who's with me in this giving revolution?

—Tobiloba

DAY 24

A Sacrifice of Praise

I was in church, and the choir sang a song about the sacrifice of praise, and it got me thinking.

Have you ever been in a place in your life where praising God was the last thing you wanted to do?

Have you ever been so angry at God that the thought of blaming God came more easily than praising Him?

If you haven't, I desire your kind of faith.

If you have, read on, my dear comrades.

You see, it is when you are in the situations above and others like it that praise becomes a sacrifice.

When you want to curse God and you praise Him instead, you are offering a sacrifice of praise.

Praise becomes a sacrifice when it costs you and goes beyond the inclinations of your natural mind. If you will have genuine faith, you will need to offer sacrifices of praise from time to time in your walk with God.

There are two distinct places in Scripture where references are made to a sacrifice of praise. They are Jeremiah 33:11 and Hebrews 13:15.

In both cases, people who were requested or admonished to offer sacrifices of praise were not exactly in the most interesting of life positions, yet God expected them to praise Him.

God understands that your praise will have to be a sacrifice sometimes. The good thing is that it is those kinds of sacrifices that are pleasing to God.

I need to be able to wholeheartedly praise God when I can't find a natural reason to.

I need to be able to offer God a sacrifice of praise.

You should do the same.

Who's with me?

—Tobiloba

DAY 25

Who's Worship?

"I just wasn't feeling today's worship. I just was not connecting," "Praise and worship was on point today", "Awesome worship."

If you are a Christian in today's world, you've probably used these exact words or words to this effect. I know I have. If you've ever been part of a choir or a worship team, you know this is how we usually give feedback after services and rehearsals.

It was during one of these feedback sessions after a Sunday service that the above question hit me.

"Who's worship? Ours or God's?" The question I'm pondering here is "Who is supposed to be enjoying worship?"

If I buy a present for a friend, I usually would buy what they would enjoy, not what I would enjoy, because it's about them.

In simple terms, worship should be a heartfelt present from us to God. Therefore the important factor here should be that God enjoys it and not necessarily that we do.

I'm not saying we should not enjoy giving the present, we should, *but* our joy should come from the fact that God is enjoying our worship and not the other way round.

How can we give God "His Worship," a worship that He would enjoy? First, we need to take our eyes off us and what appeals to our five senses, what sounds good or feels good. It is so not about us. Most of the time, we assume that once it looks or feels good to us it has to be pleasing to God.

This is not always the case. Ask Eve. The forbidden fruit looked and must have felt good too.

Note: Choir members/worship team member, this is not an excuse for lack of preparation and shoddy work! You are priests leading others to the presence of God. It is not a position to be taken lightly.

Second, we need to get to know God for ourselves. If all you know about God is what your pastor tells you, then you do not know God. You only know *about* Him. You cannot give someone a present they would appreciate if you do not know them well. Same rule applies; you cannot properly worship a God you do not know.

Think about it! You can always tell the friends that really know you by the presents they give to you for a celebration.

I'll close this with something I heard a pastor say a while back that I thought was funny but I now find rather insightful.

Worship is the only part of a Sunday service that is for God. The rest is for our benefit. Yet we take that part away by focusing on ourselves instead of on Him who should be the object of our worship.

Worship is about God. Let's not allow our (myself included) focus be subtly shifted from that goal.

Who's with me?

—Tobiloba

DAY 26

Rejoicing In Trouble

The fall of man was the beginning of the word trouble. When Jesus came to redeem us, trouble was the one thing that Jesus did not take away.

Before you crucify me and accuse me of blasphemy, I did not say it. Jesus did.

'.....in this world, you will have trouble...'- John 16:33

Trouble is an integral part of living life. Jesus identifies that. He admonishes us to expect it and tell us to even have a cheerful disposition while in trouble.

It therefore amazes me when Christians go through life expecting all things to go without hitches. Any teaching that teaches that is grossly incorrect and tends to lead people astray.

I'm not being defeatist, I'm just pointing out the truth.

What should we do when trouble comes our way? Rejoice!

I know it sounds ludicrous but that's what the word admonishes to do - James 1:2

How do you rejoice in trouble? You rejoice because you know the end of the story. Jesus tells us the end of the story- He has overcome the world.

When you know the end of the story, the twists in the plot don't faze you.

You will have trouble in this world, but you can rejoice through it.

You know the end of the story.

I can rejoice in trouble.

Who is with me?

—Tobiloba

Your Work Space, His Pulpit

I came across a reference to the calling of Peter in Luke 5:1–11 and I learned a few lessons from Peter I thought I should share.

In that story, Peter was at the end of a very long work night. I'm sure he was eager to get home. Then Jesus shows up, wanting to put the boat that was on shore already back in the water.

Talk about interruptions and additional work, but Peter obliged.

Can God interrupt your carefully orchestrated plans, or are you so set in your ways that even God can't step in and rearrange things?

Think about it.

Jesus then turned Peter's boat into His pulpit. You see Peter's boat was to him then what your work space is to you today. It was the place he earned his living, yet he allowed Jesus direct its use.

Is Jesus allowed in your work space? Can he direct the use of everything in there? Or is that one of those areas you think you can handle without him?

And the punch line of the story is the point where Jesus tells Peter where and how to fish. Peter initially objected but said the five words I love so much, "At you word, I will."

Do you allow Jesus to teach you how to do your work?

We know the end of the story.

Peter allowed his work space to become Jesus's pulpit and every known law of fishing was broken.

He never remained the same.

Jesus wants to use your work space too.

He's all you need to rewrite the law on effectiveness at work.

But you need to let him use the space first. Let him control what you do and how you do it.

I'm not talking about reeling out your day planner to God and asking Him to bless it; I'm challenging you to let God rearrange your workday.

You'll be amazed at what you'll accomplish.

Be warned though, it'll point back to Him.

Ask Peter.

I need to consciously invite God into my work space. I need to let Him run the show.

Who's with me?

—Tobiloba

DAY 28

Let Them Go

There's an adage in my language that says that "Twenty children cannot play together for twenty years.' I've found that adage to be quite true in life.

I actually confirmed that it is also a spiritual principle. There are certain things that God will not show you until certain people leave your life.

There are certain promises of God for you that will not be revealed or manifest until you separate yourself from certain people.

"In the year that King Uzziah died, I saw the Lord. He was seated on his throne. His long robe filled the temple. He was highly honoured" (Isaiah 6:1).

Every time I read that scripture, I wonder why the king had to die before Isaiah, who was a palace prophet who could see the Lord. I thought it was just conjecture until I saw another scripture and was convinced I was on the right track.

> The Lord spoke to Abram after Lot had left him. He said, "Look up from where you are. Look north and south. Look east and west. I will give you all of the land that you see. I will give it to you and your children after you forever."

Genesis 13:14–15

God waited until Lot had left Abraham before showing him what was in the plan for him.

There are certain people who need to leave your life for you to see the fullness of God and His plan for your life. Let them go.

Stop holding on to people God wants to weed out of your life before He reveals himself. Stop delaying your revelation.

Let them go! God has substitutes!

I'm letting go of unprofitable connections

Who's with me?

—Tobiloba

DAY 29

Live in Today

Every time I read the story of the "commissioning" of Moses, it always strikes me that when Moses asked how to introduce his God, God answered, "Tell them the 'I Am' sent you" (Exodus 3:13–15).

I kept thinking to myself. There are more prestigious- and high-sounding names that God could have used. Why use something related to time?

The words "I Am" in the English language is called the present tense.

Mind you, He's the one person that can go back and go forward, yet he does not refer to that ability. He chooses to stay in the present.

I thought I was going off tangent with this until I found "Before Abraham was, I Am" (John 8:58).

To me, that sounds grammatically wrong. It should have been 'I was', yet Jesus maintains the present tense even when it would have been correct on all sides to refer to the past.

What does this tell me? I need to take my cue from God and stay in the present.

A lot of the times I'm thinking of all the things that could have, would have, or should have been. I need to realise I cannot go back. It cannot be changed.

Another thing I do often is to go off thinking and thinking of what will be. I need to realise I'm not there yet. I cannot predict the future.

Little wonder the Bible admonishes us not to worry about tomorrow (Mathew 6:34).

Most of my anxieties are either over mistakes of the past or the anxieties of tomorrow.

I need to learn from the master.

I need to learn to take my cue from my present-tense father and live in today. He'll meet today's needs today and tomorrow's needs tomorrow. What's more? He deals with the past as well.

Learn from the past. Plan for the future, but please live in today.

It's the road to peace!

I choose to live in today.

So help me God.

Who's with me?

—Tobiloba

DAY 30

Silence Is Prayer Too

This week I've followed and participated in a discussion on prayer. One thing struck me that I felt I should share.

When we are asked to define prayer, everyone is quick to answer:

"Prayer is communication with God." I immediately remembered something from my "Use of English" days in the university. We were taught that communication is not complete until there is feedback.

I immediately thought about my communication with God, my prayer times.

Until a while ago, I was the only one doing all the talking whenever I decided to communicate with God. I had so much to say that God could never get a word in. As a result, my relationship with God was not growing, and I was unhappy.

Then it hit me. If I had a friend who constantly dominated the conversation every time we were talking and never let me get a word in, that relationship would probably never thrive.

Real friends listen to each other. They respect each other enough to let the other person have a say. That's how relationships grow.

To effectively communicate, you have to listen.

Quite a number of the prophets in Scripture knew this. Read with me: "**Be still all flesh before the Lord**" (Zechariah 2:13, AMP). (Stillness connotes complete silence.)

To listen you have to keep quiet. You cannot talk and listen at the same time.

In prayer, don't just talk. Listen.

To listen you have to keep quiet.

I need listen more than I talk when I pray.

Silence is prayer too.

Who's with me?

—Tobiloba

DAY 31

Honest Prayers

I just ran into the Message translation of a very common scripture, and it inspired discourse.

Read with me: "Here's what I want you to do. Find a quiet secluded place where you will not be tempted to role play before God. Just be there as simply and honestly as you can manage. The focus will shift from you to God and you will begin to sense His grace" (Matthew 6:6).

In my life, I have prayed some really dishonest prayers.

Slow down before you crucify me. You probably have too.

If you've been a Christian for a while, you will understand in a bit. Have you ever prayed a prayer by rote or from memory without giving much thought to what you were saying?

Have you ever used words in prayer just because they sounded right even though they did not reflect the true thoughts and feelings of your heart?

If you have, you've prayed dishonest prayers.

For a very long time, I was the queen of dishonest prayers. I had all the right words and inflections, but my mouth was not saying anything close to what my heart was saying.

Then a while back, God literally asked me, "Why do you think I want you to pray?"

That got me thinking. God does not need me to be His information minister. He already knows what's going on, so there's nothing I am going to tell Him that He does not already know.

So why do we think we need to pretty it up for him and sound in a certain way when we pray? He already knows what's going through our minds.

Why do we think we have to hide certain things from Him? Sorry, pal. He knows all your dirty secrets that have been hiding in the closet all these years.

Prayer should be us playing our part in building a relationship with someone who loves us by constantly communicating with Him.

If communication is to be meaningful, it has to be honest.

As humans, when we find out that someone we love has been hiding things, it hurts.

How do you think God feels every time we come to Him dishonestly?

If you're angry, tell Him.

Disappointed, hurt, scared, confused…say it as it is.

Let's stop the pretense. Let's drop the "christianese" and honestly tell God how we feel.

It will revolutionize our prayer life.
Who's with me?

—Tobiloba

Notes

God's Got Your Back
1. Hebrews 13:5, NIV

Love, Not Fear
1. 1 John 4:16–18, NLT

Is Divorce Really the Answer?
1. Mark 10, Matthew 19
2. Ephesians 5:21–33

No Marriage Is Beyond Saving
1. Mathew 19:9
2. Mathew 19:8
3. 1 Corinthians 7:11
4. Mathew 9:1

Fruit before Gifts
1. Matthew 7:15–23, MSG
2. Romans 11:29

Put Grace to Work
1. Matthew 5:20–48
2. 2 Peter 1:3, MSG
3. 1 Corinthians 15:10, MSG

Living Sacrifices
1. Romans 12:1, NIV
2. 1 Corinthians 6:19